Alice Neel, Uptown

Alice Neel, Uptown

HILTON ALS

David Zwirner Books | Victoria Miro

Contents

The Other New York | Jeremy Lewison

The working title for Hilton Als's exhibition of Alice Neel's paintings and drawings was *Colored People*.[1] It seemed to beg many questions about identity—in particular, who or what are "colored" people? His selection includes portraits of Hispanic, Japanese, African-American, Indian, and Arab men and women, among others. One immediate question is whether all of these people regard themselves as "colored" and, if they do, to what extent they see themselves in a binary relationship with whites. They surely differentiate between themselves within this grouping. Skin is a delicate affair and highly nuanced. In looking at Neel's paintings one becomes cognizant of that. Even within the black community, as portrayed by Neel, there are ethnic, attitudinal, and social differences to be noted, as well as different skin types and tones. The homogeneity implied by "colored" existed only, perhaps, in the eyes of white people. Indeed, the term was used oppressively in the era of segregation. Even now it is considered offensive since it implies that white is the default.[2] So to use such a term might appear to mark a return to outdated, racist vocabulary. But is it different if Als uses it? Can a respected African-American writer redeem a word, in the context of a discussion of Alice Neel's paintings, that hitherto has been regarded pejoratively? Can it now be used to describe the complexity and variety of her subjects?

In American society during Neel's lifetime, "colored"[3] was certainly considered *other*, but for Neel herself, everyone was equal in all their idiosyncrasies and racial differences. Everyone was a member of her club. She painted people no matter what their color, creed, or social standing, and this is what makes her oeuvre so unique. It is singular in the sense that no other major artist had done that, but it is varied in its breadth of subject.

However, painting individuals that were commonly referred to as "colored people" has a wider significance than just capturing the faces and personalities of those who surrounded her.

If there is one subject underpinning Neel's work of the 1940s and 1950s, it was her desire to paint what Michael Harrington was to call "the other America" in his eponymous book, published in 1962.[4] Written as a complement to John Kenneth Galbraith's 1958 best-selling publication *The Affluent Society*,[5] Harrington, and indeed Galbraith, pointed out the enormous and growing gap between rich and poor in the United States, which, they believed, only state intervention could mitigate. In the urban situation, the poor were predominantly immigrants, African-Americans, and Hispanics.

One cannot claim that Neel was as poor as many of her neighbors in Spanish Harlem, since she received handouts from supporters and patrons from time to time, but she knew what hardship was like and she observed it in her everyday contacts. Neel was part of the beat generation, described by Harrington as the "voluntary" poor.[6] They lived in tenements among the impoverished, with very few resources, but unlike the black population living in nearby Harlem, these middle-class, university-educated literati chose this way of life in rebellion against the "affluent society."[7] They were not victims.

Harrington describes poverty in areas of urban deprivation—in particular Harlem[8]—as an issue that could not be remedied by dealing with one single aspect. It needed to be addressed as a whole. The population of the inner-city ghettos had little chance of escape since it was by and large excluded from white-dominated educational facilities. Black people, he said, were also to a large extent politically invisible. As Harrington describes it, the affluent middle classes moved out to suburbia and simply passed through the ghettos on the train or the drive into town, averting their eyes. Ralph Ellison had already enshrined this invisibility in his novel *Invisible Man*, which won the National Book Award for fiction in 1953. "I am invisible . . . simply because people refuse to see me," the unnamed and undescribed narrator establishes at the beginning of Ellison's novel.[9] It seems strange, however, that Harrington persisted in regarding African-Americans as invisible at precisely the time when the civil rights movement was in full swing. While it is true, as he states, that they had little political representation, by 1962, African-Americans were increasingly vocal and were representing themselves outside the formal institutions.

Harrington's remedy, beyond a federal solution, was for the poor to become visible through culture: "The poor can be described statistically," he wrote; "they can be analyzed as a group. But they need a novelist as well as a sociologist if we are to see them. They need an American Dickens to record the smell and texture and quality of their lives."[10]

Alice Neel was no Dickens. She did not narrate epic stories, just as she was not really Balzac in spite of her claim to have painted an equivalent to *La Comédie humaine*. But she did observe, in her own dynamic and sensitive way, the specifics of the poverty and people that surrounded her in Spanish Harlem, as well as the community's black activist writers and intellectual leaders. Smell, texture, and quality of life are exactly what she recorded.

She moved to Spanish Harlem just after the heyday of the Harlem Renaissance, so we should not be fooled into thinking she was cut off from a cultural environment. Her milieu, with a substantial communist inflection, was intellectual, compassionate, and suffused with creative and socially active people. On the one hand, her empathy

for Harrington's so-called "victims" is apparent in many drawings and paintings, as well as the dignity with which they bore their burdens. *Black Spanish-American Family* is a fine example, where the sitters appear to be dressed in their Sunday best.[11] But she also captured the sense of threat that came with growing up in that rough environment; the transformation, for example, of Georgie Arce from angelic child to knife-bearing adolescent.[12] On the other hand, she also was aware of intellectual and political foment: she portrayed Horace R. Cayton, the eminent African-American sociologist who wrote about working-class black Americans, particularly in Chicago;[13] Harold Cruse, an outspoken racial critic who became a university academic and was a co-founder, with Amiri Baraka (then known as LeRoi Jones), of the Black Arts Repertory Theatre and School in Harlem;[14] Hubert Satterfield, a communist writer; and Alvin Simon, a young writer, all of whom would have been considered middle or upper middle class.

She lived, however, in the Hispanic community. Among her subjects were the ordinary people she met regularly; the tradesmen, the shopkeepers, the artisans, the children playing in the street, and the members of her wider family, the Negrons, whom she painted on multiple occasions. She depicted the pride with which they inhabited their bodies as well as the discomfort. Above all, Neel's sitters were not sociological statistics but human beings whose individuality of color, bearing, and demeanor she captured. These were not the kind of people she had encountered in Greenwich Village, where she had lived a bohemian life in the 1930s, but were specific to the environment of Spanish Harlem.

After she moved to the Upper West Side, just south of Harlem proper, in 1962,[15] she had a different experience among the educated classes in the neighborhood of Columbia University. Poverty and local community were no longer her subjects, and the few African-Americans, Asians, or non-white people who sat for her then had achieved a certain social status. Peter Kanuthia was an African businessman, Ron Kajiwara a graphic designer for *Vogue*, and Abdul Rahman a taxi driver. Her portraits of James Farmer and his children, both done in the mid-1960s, however, were not simply a throwback to interests of the Spanish Harlem years, but a strong political statement. Farmer worked alongside Martin Luther King Jr. to dismantle segregation by means of nonviolent protest and was one of the main instigators of the Freedom Rides in 1961 and the March on Washington for Jobs and Freedom in 1963. For a white woman to paint Farmer in 1964 was an act of defiance and commitment to the cause.

If there was an essential darkness to the Spanish Harlem works, where her palette seemed to reflect or represent the material hardship of the times with a certain pathos, there was a complete change in tone after moving to the Upper West Side. Neel's paintings became filled with light and permeated with optimism, as though her belief in the goodness of humanity had won through. Perhaps, also, she had overcome her own depression.[16]

But Neel went on to record another section of the downtrodden, one that was classless and in the throes of protesting for equality. The women's movement took off almost immediately after the civil rights movement made its greatest gains. Neel began to focus more on women and families than in previous years. Her concentration on the nature of women's lives was as unprecedented as her depiction of the New York constituents of Harrington's "other America." In fact, in the 1960s, one might argue that women formed another part of the "other America," the overlooked and the oppressed. This was the final piece in Neel's account of the other New York.

Notes

1. The final title of the exhibition is *Alice Neel, Uptown*, referring to Neel's years living in Spanish Harlem and the Upper West Side.
2. The actor Benedict Cumberbatch had to apologize for carelessly using the term "colored" when referring to black actors in an interview on PBS's *Tavis Smiley* show on January 21, 2015.
3. In Neel's lifetime "colored" was the word that replaced "negro," which was too close to the term of abuse used by slave owners. But that term too became a tool of oppression and segregation.
4. Michael Harrington, *The Other America: Poverty in the United States* (New York: Macmillan, 1962; Baltimore: Penguin Books, 1967).
5. John Kenneth Galbraith, *The Affluent Society* (Boston: Houghton Mifflin, 1958). The book was reprinted four times in the same year.
6. See Harrington, *The Other America* (1967), pp. 84–88.
7. Harrington used the term "negro" to describe the African-American population, to differentiate them from other non-white people.
8. Harrington, *The Other America* (1967), p. 63. Harrington refers to Harlem as an "urban slum," and nominates it the "negro capital" of America.
9. Ralph Ellison, *Invisible Man* (New York: Random House, 1952), p. 3.
10. Harrington, *The Other America* (1967), p. 24.
11. The complex racial title was not given by Neel but was subsequently applied.
12. Arce would later be imprisoned for homicide.
13. In 1945, Cayton coauthored, with St. Clair Drake, the important study *Black Metropolis: A Study of Negro Life in a Northern City*, which was based on research done in Chicago, primarily under the auspices of the Works Progress Administration. At the time Neel painted him, four years later, he was director of the Parkway Community House in Chicago, or had just left its employment.
14. According to William J. Maxwell, Cruse, who was a member of the Communist Party, was recruited as an informer by the FBI. See Maxwell, *F.B. Eyes: How J. Edgar Hoover's Ghostreaders Framed African American Literature* (Princeton: Princeton University Press, 2015), p. 106.
15. Neel's move was precipitated by her landlord, who wanted to vacate and renovate the building in Spanish Harlem where she had lived from 1942 to 1962.
16. After her relationship with Sam Brody ended Neel sought psychological help. Her self-portrait drawing as a skull may testify to her state of mind at the end of the 1950s.

People on Steps, 1952

Introduction | Hilton Als

I grew up in Brooklyn. For a while, on weekends, my father would take me and my little brother into "the city." My father loved to walk, and he loved foreign films and foreign food. This meant that we saw different areas of Manhattan all the time. We ate sauerkraut in Germantown on the Upper East Side, and bought brisket and bialys on the Lower East Side. Looking back now, I can see that my father showed us as much of the world as he could without going out into the actual world, or beyond Brooklyn and Manhattan. I think anything outside the parameters of what he knew—he sought the unfamiliar in the familiar—felt dangerous to him and so, presumably, to his male children, whom he could not love; he had an aversion to maleness. Daddy was the only son of West Indian immigrants, and it occurs to me now that all those places we visited with him, down in Chinatown and beyond, were some version of his immigrant experience—a world of strivers gathered around their native food, trading stories about the new world. I suppose my brother and I were, to some extent, representative of the new world. In any case, visiting those various neighborhoods in Manhattan prepared us for many things, including the feeling that different people were not unfamiliar to us; when you're a child, the world is oneself. Still, there were signs that this feeling of oneness would not remain forever. My mother raised me, my brother, and one of my older sisters on welfare. This was during the time when social workers could come to your house to see if you had anything you shouldn't have, like a husband, or a television. Something in my heart, though, concentrated on this feeling of oneness I wanted to have with someone, and with the world. Determination was, for a time, my very soul.

When I was ten or eleven, I began to go out into the world with my little brother. On Saturday afternoons, we crawled under the turnstile and jumped on the subway—we had no money to speak of—and went to Brooklyn Heights. (We lived in Crown Heights.) Our father had taken us to that beautiful neighborhood; we'd sit on the promenade and look out at the river, sketching boats while he read the paper. I believe he liked to be alone just as I like to be alone, but he wanted that isolation without our love, while I never want to do without love, even when I want to be alone. Brooklyn Heights was my dream of life. There was the water and a view of "the city," and I remember forsythia; I remember how, once, while I was looking at those beautiful little blooms, Norman Mailer passed us and nodded, and was kind. Undoubtedly he was interested in how two colored boys got there. This was in the early 1970s, before children were abducted and never heard from again.

I was six or seven when I began taking the subway by myself. I asked my mother if I could—my older sister made me late for school and I didn't like being late for school. It strikes me as odd now when people are surprised by this, and it never occurred to me then that children might require a certain degree of protection. I still don't quite know what it means to be a child, the reception of guidance and protectiveness. I don't know what that means. I loved my mother and she trusted me to get to where I needed to go.

Those Brooklyn Heights trips with my brother were but a prelude to going into the city. I realize now that I was emulating my father, the best part of him. That's one way kids show their love and try to get love: by saying, Look, I'm just like you! When I walked with my brother, I held his hand like my father held my hand, or like how I wanted him to hold my hand. I wanted my father's love for sure, but I wasn't like my father. (Eventually I would have a fantasy of love with men who bore some emotional resemblance to him.) Once, on the phone, he told my mother that he objected to me going into the city. When my mother had had enough, she said, But you exposed him to all of that. I suppose I'm not the first child, or the last, to make a parent angry by taking the best part of that parent's self and doing something positive with it. Maybe my father thought I was "besting" him, not loving him, when I got on that subway. It occurs to me now, too, that when I began making those trips with my brother, I no longer had to wait for my father to take me any place.

My mother was a reader. She loved Paule Marshall's *Brown Girl, Brownstones*. When I found out, somehow, that Marshall lived in the city, I telephoned the operator, got her number, and called her up. I told her all about my mother and how much we loved her books. She had her son get on the extension. When my mother came home, she found me sleeping by the phone; when I told her about the call, she thought I'd been dreaming. But there was proof: I had written Marshall's number down, and her address, silently determined that I would get there one day. That day came soon enough. Not too long after I had that conversation with Marshall, I figured out how to get to her home, in East Harlem. After getting off at the wrong stop, I walked for what seemed like a long time to get to her apartment building. On the walk I passed through street scenes that were not unlike the scenes I saw back in Crown Heights: families cooling it on stoops, kids making rainbows in open fire hydrants. None of this jibed with what I imagined about Marshall. She was an author and therefore her world should be, I thought, cleaner, more orderly, glamorous. But here she was, living in a world that was not unlike mine. Did being an artist mean living in a ghetto for one's art? When would the world be different? When I finally reached her apartment building and went upstairs, the grime and harsh light and kids screaming in the apartments beyond were not unfamiliar to me. I had arrived at a place I knew. When I knocked on her door and asked to see her, a woman said, from behind that door, that Marshall wasn't home. The woman had a strong West Indian accent: her mother, another real-life source for the complicated matriarchs in her books. Was this art? The real voice behind the door? Was this what I had to make art out of—a reality I didn't want to know? My father, those little apartments we lived in with my mother, the place I grew up in and longed to get out of: Was this to be a source of art? How to render things realistically if one wasn't a realist of the heart?

I believe that one reason I began writing essays—a form without a form, until you make it—was this: you didn't have to borrow from an emotionally and visually upsetting past, as one did in fiction, apparently, to write your story. In an essay, your story could include your actual story and even more stories; you could collapse time and chronology and introduce other voices. In short, the essay is not about the empirical "I" but about the collective—all the voices that made your "I." When I first saw Alice Neel's pictures, I think I recognized a similar ethos of inclusion in her work. The pictures were a collaboration, a pouring in of energy from both sides—the sitter's and the artist's. This was very unusual, then and now—so many artists are so terrifically invested in their "I" that they feel the world would disappear if not for it. Neel, on the other hand, believed the world existed on its own terms, and it was our duty—as citizens, as artists—to know as much about it as possible, in order to better live in it and navigate it; to exist among all the broken glass and bottle caps and boys on the street, in a kind of unsentimental wonder. The world does not need our sentimentality, Neel's portraits seem to say, but our interest and empathy; those two qualities are very hard to focus and manage, if you are even capable of it at all.

I didn't know, when I went to pay homage to Marshall that long-ago early evening in East Harlem, that Neel had lived nearby for many years. But it makes a kind of sense. Marshall wrote about what she called the "poets in the kitchen"—all those immigrant women who told the tales she remembered and remade in her fiction. Neel, looking at those immigrant women in East Harlem, let them be just as she rendered them, through her vision, concern, and interest. Neel was not a sentimentalist, but you can tell where her concerns were: with those people who didn't have the means to speak for themselves. It wasn't that she always loved her East Harlem subjects, but you can always tell when she was turned on by them—by their physicality, mind, or interiority. She didn't hide from the erotics of looking. Again, this was—and still is—very unusual for a woman, whose social responsibility it is, we've been told, to keep the family (society) together, which requires silence. But Neel would speak. She would not only speak, but she would speak in tandem with those who didn't see the value of speaking out—after all, the world had spoken against *them.*

Might one call Neel a kind of essayist of the canvas? When I first saw her work—this might have been in the late 1970s, when I was not yet twenty—I was immediately consumed by the stories she worked so hard to tell: about loneliness, togetherness, and the drama of self-presentation, spurred by the drama of being. Years passed, and I continued to look at Neel. What struck me about her vast oeuvre, after a while, was all the people of color she painted. This was unusual, and is still. The truth of the matter is that many—most—contemporary artists of non-color are interested in reflecting themselves, their creamy whiteness and hair untroubled by thought. On the flip side, many artists of color who make a buck nowadays do it by equating blackness with oppression and selling the result to white people without feeling a thing for their subjects' lives. Neel's work smashes both of those categories, showing us the humanness embedded in subjects that people might classify as "different." I really think that Neel's marginalization by curators like Henry Geldzahler had to do with the fact that she painted different people. Did that not make her different, too? Had Neel restricted her canvas to the white world, she would have been celebrated sooner, swear to God, because then her detractors, or the people who ignored or marginalized her, would have seen themselves, which, in the art world at least, is always rewarded. That wasn't who Alice Neel, artist, was though. She did not treat colored people as an ideological cause, either, but as a point of interest in the life she was leading there, in East Harlem and beyond. Sometimes when I look at Neel's work, I imagine the people she would have painted had she lived to paint them. My father would have been one of her guys. He was very handsome, remote, and troubled. Imagine what Alice would have drawn out of him, simply—and complicatedly—because she was interested in his looks, his skin, and the world beyond his skin? Her essay would have succeeded where, just now, I've failed.

Girl with Pink Flower, 1940s

Baby on Blue Sofa, 1939–1940

Two Girls in Spanish Harlem, 1941

Julie and the Doll, 1943

Alice Neel moved to Spanish Harlem with her Puerto Rican lover, José Negron, a singer, in 1938. Their first address: 8 East 107th Street. By the time she emigrated north, Neel had tired of her life downtown and considered Greenwich Village "a honky-tonk." We all find the world we need to live in—the better to be ourselves and find a little comfort. For Neel, that world was Spanish Harlem, with its manifest "difference," its ties to José's culture, and her love of that culture. Not many white women artists lived in that neighborhood then. It didn't take Neel, with her reportorial eye, long to see that her milieu was relatively uncharted territory, and that there, in that world of music and bodegas and sadness and hope, her politics and identification with the "underclass" had found a home. As a young art student at the Philadelphia School of Design for Women, Neel bristled against how art was used, and why. "There were all these rich girls who went there as a finishing school," Neel said about her alma mater. "At the start I went out to lunch with them, but I realized that wasn't what I was there for, so I gave up everything and became a grind. . . . I worked so hard because I had a conscience about going to art school. Not for my own family, but for all the poor in the world. Because when I'd go into the school, the scrubwomen would be coming back from scrubbing office floors all night. It killed me that these old gray-headed women had to scrub floors, and I was going in there to draw Greek statues."

Politics are borne of conscience and feeling and not a little identification. When she moved to New York from her native Pennsylvania, Neel saw more of the world—and what made people different in the world. She looked for language that might describe those feelings to herself and others. She read and quoted W.E.B. Du Bois, and, later in life, when she was lecturing fairly regularly, she did not disguise her anger if she noticed that the students knew next to nothing about current events. "How can you be an artist and not know what's going on in the world?" the sculptor Robert Gober recalls her saying to his fellow students when he was in art school. Of course, part of Neel's greatness lies in the fact that art for her didn't have an ideological function, but it could be informed by a particular point of view. Look at her portraits of people in East Harlem, and then look at the paintings she made of outsiders in the 1970s. *Julie and the Doll* is as richly textured with understanding as Neel's 1970 *Jackie Curtis and Ritta Redd.* Each touches on similar themes: isolation, self-presentation, the strength and fracture that go into being a marginalized self or so-called marginal self. Every artist works alone, a necessity that is both the burden and joy of making art: there are no others, only you. Only you can tell this story. Neel tells Julie's story—the story of a community—in canvas after canvas, each one startling and distinct. Neel was profound in her understanding of community: it emerges from the individual, not the group.

In 1942, Neel moved with her sons, Richard and Hartley, to 21 East 108th Street. This was to be the family home for the next twenty years. Meanwhile, downstairs, on the street, the Brooklyn-born photographer Helen Levitt was taking pictures of the kids making a theater out of those East Harlem avenues. (Levitt was thirteen years younger than Neel.) Her photographs of chalk drawings, city youths, stoops, weather, and atmosphere had a number of fans, including the writer James Agee. Neel had no such critical support; indeed, most of the years she lived at East 108th Street were spent in relative isolation. Still, it's interesting to consider these two women—both of whom were "different" than the world they recorded—in light of their politics and what their eye responded to. Like Neel, Levitt was a leftist and was cynical in her view of power. In East Harlem, she found what Agee called an "aesthetic reality." As a photographer, Levitt edited the scene to find its essence, its story. Neel worked with the real to reinterpret it as her reality; she was not a documentarian. While she had to work from a *felt* distance in order to paint her subject's interiority, with all its fluctuations, she knew the truth when she saw it, too.

The camera's eye and the painter's hand are different. The former takes life as it comes, in an instant, but can be described as a series of selective moments. Painting, on the other hand, has time on its side, the better to know, delve, and express what it's like for two people to sit in a room, observing one another while talking or not talking about the world. Levitt was different than most documentary photographers; like Diane Arbus, she went back to her subjects again and again, the better to understand who they were, and who they were in relation to herself. Her pictures of East Harlem show how that world changes, especially in relation to its inhabitants: poverty becomes more glaring, the neighborhood disperses. In the paintings Neel made at East 108th

Street, it's the breakdown of the subject—because of the changes in the outside world—that remains so startling. Her subjects sit upright while they crumble. They remain stalwart in their determination to *be*, and to hold on to what they have—even if it's a doll, as dead as anything, but alive, too, because of the love and possessiveness a child like Julie confers on it—even if the world would rather not know them or anything about them. Alice Neel's paintings fight against the status quo's determined stance to forget the living whom they feel contribute nothing to their lives, even as they make so much life around them.

The Spanish Family, 1943

T.B. Harlem, 1940

Building in Harlem, c. 1945

There was no portrait that day, but there would be paint. There was no agony of expression to observe that day, but there would be paint. No twisted or joyful limb, no trinity of girls with mourning eyes to draw that day, but there would be paint. Maybe she saw the building from, or near, her building, which was on East 108th Street. It was 1945 or so. The only thing we can report with any degree of accuracy at all is the year *Building in Harlem* was painted, and where the apartments were—uptown, in Harlem. All else is conjecture. She was a portraitist down to her bones. So when she saw the building, maybe she saw a face; the building tilts a little, like a human head in repose. It sags a little, too, maybe reflecting the spiritual weight of its inhabitants—colored people, mostly, or most likely, given that it was Harlem during the war, or right after. Many of the colored people Alice Neel lived near in Spanish Harlem were Puerto Rican, Cuban, or Dominican, all hoping for a better day amidst old ways—the old colonial ways from back home, centuries before, when the Spanish had colonized them, given them a different tongue, thus removing them further from their African ways and Indian roots. Now, tree roots are trying to break through the concrete in East Harlem—the very same pavement the Latin boys are standing on in their sneakers in *Building in Harlem*—just guys shooting the shit under clouds that don't overwhelm the image, but help make it.

During the course of her productive, complicated, and free life, Neel made many portraits. Sometimes they were in words, such as this poem, which further articulates the love she had for place, faces, the spiritual body within the body:

> I love you Harlem
> Your life your pregnant
> Women, your relief lines
> Outside the bank, full
> Of women who no dress
> In Saks 5th Ave would
> Fit, teeth missing, weary,
> Out of shape, little black
> Arms around their necks

Clinging to their skirts
All the wear and worry
Of struggle on their faces
What a treasure of goodness
And life shambles
Thru the streets,
Abandoned, despised,
Charged the most, given
The worst
I love you for electing
Marcantonio, and him
For being what he is
And for the rich deep vein
Of human feeling buried
Under your fire engines
Your poverty and your loves

Harlem was her home. There was struggle, but goodness in the struggle, and there was poverty and love, too. As a single mother of two trying to make ends meet, she recognized the struggle on her neighbors' faces, because children clung to her skirts, wrapped their arms around her neck as well. She was needed and was needy. She would not wait to see if it was "appropriate" to diversify or not—to be part of a community that was not supposed to be her own, as a white woman, an educated girl from Pennsylvania who had all sorts of chances, but so few chances, too. No matter what, she was a woman—she would just do it. Because East Harlem was what she felt like, or identified with, no matter what she looked like. Neel knew the difference between self-presentation—the self one showed to the world, or the self the world saw first and inevitably judged, based on skin color, sex, whatever—and what the soul looked like to itself. And, on some level, Neel's soul saw itself in East Harlem, where struggle contributed to the making of faces, along with goodness, while all that life shambled through the streets.

Building in Harlem is a vertical picture. The image rises up just as hope rises up. Had Neel wanted to make a different picture—a picture of urban despair, say—she wouldn't have painted that sky, or those socially engaged boys. She would have focused on that sagging building, an emblem of difference housing difference. But she always pulled back from the predictable, if she even knew what that was: the East Harlem she saw and lived in for forty years, and raised a family in, was not, to her eye and heart, a sociological problem, a valley of statistics filled with the dispossessed. Instead, it was a place filled, at times, with light, sky, street-corner jive, buildings as haunted and full as the people she sought to paint in her portraits—those portraits she would get back to tomorrow after she finished building *Building in Harlem*, which has a face of its own.

Armando Perez, 1945

Horace Cayton, 1949

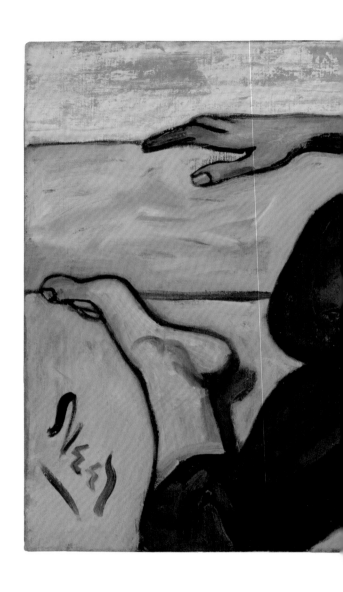

Ballet Dancer, 1950

Rudolph Christian, 1951

Georgie Arce, 1955

Then there's Georgie. Georgie Arce, a kid from the neighborhood. By the looks of him, he was trouble, or trouble in the making. Alice Neel was attracted to the drama of being, so how could she resist what Georgie was willing to give? All that brazen turmoil in one so young, who was not so young. (Georgie eventually became a con artist, a street guy; in 1974, he was convicted on two counts of murder and one count of conspiracy to commit murder.) In truth, Neel's portraits of Georgie are not really pictures of a kid—of youth evolving into maturity—so much as they're images describing masculinity, or a particular kind of masculinity that tapped into her eros. It's eros that informs the shape and size of Georgie's hands (much too big for a child, but big enough for a powerful man); his large, dramatic head; his sneering, relaxed, leering mouth. He is, to some extent, the son of the preening José, one of Neel's lovers in the 1930s and father of her oldest boy, Richard. But he's José with a different kind of self-regard—none of that artistic "sensitivity"—mixed with a Spanish-influenced machismo, which Neel captured in simultaneously romantic and reportorial detail. (Neel's portraits of José—who, like Georgie, was Puerto Rican—remind one of V.S. Naipaul's gripping descriptions of louche machismo in 1970s Argentina.) The surrounding atmosphere in the Arce portraits is almost without exception dark; apparently Neel's apartment on East 108th Street, where the majority of the Georgie pictures were made, was not well lit. That darkness might have encouraged a certain degree of transference from artist to subject, and back again: the dim light allowed for a certain amount of dream space, or distance. The Georgie pictures are dense with the force of his personality, his arrogance, and his movie-star desire to be looked at. He has the hair of a heartthrob; Sal Mineo could have played him in a movie.

In one interview, Neel described herself as "inhibited." Often women feel constrained by certain social responsibilities—to be a "woman," which is to say controlled, a maker of home, not a disrupter or destroyer of it. In Georgie, Neel found an uninhibited male—there are many in her gallery, ranging from her famous 1933 portrait of Joe Gould, to the fascinating 1935 picture of writer Max White, to her 1962 painting *Robert Smithson*, jittery with energy. Georgie, and all the others, could do socially what she, as a woman, could not do, or had been trained not to do: parade a kind of arrogance or self-delight in being before an audience of one or many. Neel's Georgie portraits are exercises in the erotics of style. Georgie, by virtue of his sex and wiliness, acts out as Neel reflects on his acting out. She takes him in and he moves toward her, moves towards the viewer as if to say, so, what are you going to do about it? Her Georgie pictures ask: What is masculinity? What is machismo? Is it cultural? Or "just" unique to the individual? And what does that make me, Alice Neel? A "woman"? What is that? The eyes that give masculinity the stage it requires to wreck and build homes, almost simultaneously?

Georgie, 1950

Georgie Arce, 1952

Georgie Arce, 1953

A Spanish Boy, 1955

Georgie Arce, 1955

Georgie Arce, 1959

Georgie, 1958

Georgie Arce No. 2, 1955

Alice Childress, 1950

Alice Childress, author and playwright, would have been in her mid-thirties when Alice Neel painted this picture of her. Aside from the flowers, the table they're resting on, a chair cushion, and part of a window frame, Childress fills the canvas; a light-skinned woman of color, she wears her authority like a cloak and her hat like a crown. When I was a boy, there was a book service at my school, and every month you'd sign up for a new story. One book I requested and loved was Childress's novel, *A Hero Ain't Nothin' but a Sandwich*. Published in 1973, it tells the story of Benjie, a thirteen-year-old black kid who gets hooked on heroin. I was a kid when I read it, and to this day I can recall the horror and sadness I felt as I pored over those pages; it was like looking at the world I grew up in, when so many boys my age didn't make it. Cities were on fire with drugs, and Harlem was just another dumping ground for the poison. Neel lived in East Harlem until 1962, so she was an eyewitness to the downfall; it would not be out of the realm of possibility for her to have known, during that time, somebody's child she'd watched growing up on the streets of East Harlem end up in trouble, strung out on drugs.

Throughout her work, Childress captured the pathos of change and its humor, too. Around the same time I read *Hero*, I saw producer and director Joseph Papp's 1974 television adaptation of Childress's phenomenal play, *Wedding Band: A Love/Hate Story in Black and White*. Set at the outset of the First World War, the play's ostensible theme was miscegenation in the South (Childress was born in South Carolina and raised in Harlem), but race is only part of the social fabric of the story. At its heart is love—love's impossibilities, and the frightening rewards and ruptures that occur when you lay your body down next to an equally vulnerable soul. Childress had yet to write any of these works in 1950, though. She was, however, a long-standing member of the American Negro Theatre, known for her acting. (She was nominated for a Tony for her role in Philip Yordan's all-black show, *Anna Lucasta*, in 1944.) And she had started to write. Her debut piece, the one-act play *Florence*, produced in 1949, is still interesting to read because it expresses what Childress continued to explore in her mature dramatic work: what it felt like to be an artist of color and a woman in a world that had very little use for either.

I'm sure Neel would have known Childress through their various political associations; Neel, a former member of the WPA, would have known that the American Negro Theatre was founded under the aegis of the Negro Unit of the Federal Theatre Project in Harlem. In a sense, Childress and Neel were sisters, certainly when it came to their experience of the government taking an active interest in the lives of artists. Plus, they both loved Harlem. (Childress lived there for most of her professional life.) When I think of Neel's portrait of her fellow artist, the word aspiration comes to mind. Childress looks out onto a world that's real, and out of that reality she, like Neel, will make the most of her vision and alchemy. Thinking of Neel and Childress in the artist's studio, one imagines a play Childress didn't write—a play in which the subject and the artist talk about what their bodies must bear in order to represent intimacy in all its forms, like now, as Neel's brush hits the canvas and Childress, in an act of modesty and dreaming, turns away from the artist's eye while turning inward to look at her own.

Spanish Woman, c. 1950

Black Spanish-American Family, 1950

Harold Cruse, c. 1950

Harold Cruse published *The Crisis of the Negro Intellectual*, his magnum opus, in 1967, by which time the civil rights movement had given way to black nationalism, exemplified by the Black Panther Party and other organizations. Cruse was a man of action. Born in Virginia, he was raised in New York; after high school he served in the army during World War II; after returning from Europe, he attended the City College of New York and became a member of the Communist Party. That association lasted for several years, after which time he co-founded, with the poet Amiri Baraka, the Black Arts Repertory Theatre and School in Harlem. Cruse always loved the stage. A favorite aunt used to take him to shows when he was growing up, but he felt the commercial theater underrepresented people of color; he thought that blacks, Hispanics, Native Americans, and others should tell their own stories and be, to some extent, culturally self-governing. Cruse's most famous book began as a talk; it grew, and grows in the mind. His portraits of black intellectuals ranging from Richard Wright to Lorraine Hansberry to James Baldwin, in addition to his analysis of Jewish liberals and black politics, remain incredibly powerful and agitating. Cruse was not a stylist the way that Alice Neel was a stylist; his voice is not about nuance but building an argument. Beauty was not his project; his aim was to describe what had happened to black America in the cradle of modernism— Harlem in the 1920s, and after.

Neel was a woman of action, too. She knew that politics was synonymous with movement, with exercising one's critical intelligence. In 1971, she picketed the Whitney Museum of American Art, protesting its lack of inclusion of black art experts in the curatorial process. There's a photograph of Neel on that picket line. It's winter, and she's marching in a cold sun, holding her placard right below her heart. This was only three years before the Whitney mounted its retrospective of her work, but one gets the sense that while she needed her work to be shown, she was, for all her life, skeptical about institutions. What links Neel's gallery of souls is their accelerated feeling, be it about their art, their family, their clothing, their difference. Cruse must have interested her because he was involved in ideas that involved her home—Harlem—just as she was interested in it because of what it gave her: ideas wrapped in being.

Mercedes Arroyo, 1952

Three Puerto Rican Girls, 1955

Two Puerto Rican Boys, 1956

Two Girls, 1954

In her phenomenal 1961 study, *The Death and Life of Great American Cities*,
Jane Jacobs wrote of her horror of the corporate planning and Le Corbusier—
inspired building that was then threatening to take over her beloved downtown
New York. Spearheaded by the developer Robert Moses—who, for example,
proposed the destruction of what we now know as SoHo to accommodate a super
highway—the planners' proposed changes would have done nothing to support
or enhance what Jacobs loved about Manhattan, and what Manhattan loved
about itself: its neighborhoods, filled with street life, and its citizens' ethnic,
religious, and sexual differences. In his introduction to the fiftieth anniversary
edition of the text, Jason Epstein, Jacobs's editor, wrote that "unlike Detroit or
Pittsburgh, New York was not defined by a dominant industry. New York was a
cornucopia of possibility and improvisation, an incubator of vital neighborhoods
and local citizenship."

Alice Neel painted her local citizenship, up in East Harlem and, later, on the
Upper West Side. So doing, she recorded what Jacobs considered essential to
the life of the city: diversity. Jacobs wrote: "In our American cities, we need all
kinds of diversity, intricately mingled in mutual support. We need this so city
life can work decently and constructively, and so the people of cities can sustain
(and further develop) their society and civilization." In short, Jacobs viewed
diversity as a civilizing influence; dealing with that which you are not—or do not
think you are—in areas that are self-defining (i.e., neighborhoods where stores
cater to the culinary needs of "foreign" clients, and so on) not only educates
one about difference, but encourages those differences to flourish. Jacobs said
that city planning should pay attention to social nuances, any social nuances,
because then "city districts will be economically and socially congenial places
for diversity to generate itself and reach its best potential if the districts possess
good mixtures of primary uses, frequent streets, a close-grained mingling of
different ages in their buildings, and a high concentration of people."

Neel was a painter of modern life, and part of her genius was based on
her knowledge and embrace of the fact that New York was not a homogenous
place; she knew there were many different kinds of stories to tell when she sat
in front of that canvas. *Two Girls* shows diversity within diversity—"ethnic"

girls from different places, but together, in Harlem, with Neel in her home there. It is a work of great intimacy, but one could say that about Neel's work in general, certainly the best of it. By the time Neel made this painting, East Harlem was considered a ghetto; a portion of it was being leveled to make way for housing projects, or the hideously termed "urban renewal." (In 1960, James Baldwin published a powerful essay about this phenomenon. In "Fifth Avenue, Uptown," the great author describes his Harlem childhood, and the destruction of his poverty-stricken neighborhood when "the projects" were built; history and personality were exchanged for uniform, industrialized poverty.) Formerly known as Italian Harlem, Neel's East 108th Street locale and its environs had been, at one point, a hub for late nineteenth-century Italian-American life—when Italian immigrants had joined the poor Irish, Polish, and so on, who made uneasy room for their darker European relations. During this time, the Italian-American mafia became a force; New York's future mayor, Fiorello H. La Guardia, represented Italian Harlem in Congress in the 1930s. But things change because cities change. After World War I, Puerto Rican and Latin American immigrants flooded the city; a number congregated on the western side of East Harlem—around 110th Street and Lexington Avenue. The Italians began moving out—to the suburbs, to the Bronx. There was another wave of Puerto Rican immigrants in the 1940s and 1950s; when you said you lived in "El Barrio"—"The Neighborhood"—New Yorkers knew what you meant. Neel paints that world not as a ghetto, but as a universe filled with many, many different kinds of stories. One senses in the work from this period that the artist was incredibly respectful, without being sentimental or laudatory, about the world that opened itself up to her and her children. It's a rapidly vanishing world; developers move in and buildings, neighborhoods change again. The East Harlem that Neel depicted shifts its focus from renters to owners, from difference to those who can afford to eradicate difference; perhaps it will now become subject to the kind of success Jacobs warned against when she wrote that success destroys diversity:

> This, in broad strokes, is what happens: A diversified mixture of uses at some place in the city becomes outstandingly popular and successful as a whole. Because of the location's success, which is invariably based on flourishing and magnetic diversity, ardent competition for space in

this locality develops. It is taken up in what amounts to the economic equivalent of a fad. . . . If tremendous numbers of people, attracted by convenience and interest, or charmed by vigor and excitement, choose to live or work in the area, again the winners of the competition will form a narrow segment of population of users. Since so many want to get in, those who get in or stay in will be self-sorted by the expense.

Neel did not want to get in, and if someone perceived that was her impulse for anything other than her art—getting into a subject—she would fight to get out. Whether she was drawing *Two Girls*, or any number of other subjects in El Barrio, the theme was diversity not calling attention to itself, but being what it was: part of her subject's self, the poetry she excavated on East 108th Street and after, day after day.

Young Woman, 1956

Nurse, 1954

Rita and Hubert, 1958

Two Girls, Spanish Harlem, 1959

Call Me Joe, 1955

When I was in Los Angeles recently, the poet Robin Coste Lewis taught me about erasure. I had never heard of this before. Developed—but is that the word?—in the 1960s by poets and artists like Doris Cross, erasure poetry is picked out from text that has come before. Here's how: you take some words from, say, Virginia Woolf's *The Voyage Out*, and find, in her thousands of sentences, a much shorter verse—a poem of one's own. So, instead of a line that reads, "Yes, she knew she must go back to all that, but at present she must weep," the erasure might read: "Go back, weep." And that would be one line, which would connect to another erased line, and so on.

It is important to live with voids, with absences. I am drawn to this way of thinking because, as life progresses, there are more and more voids, and they are more painful without something—some meaning—to anchor the spirit in this spiritless arena of loss. The great tragic event of my life is AIDS; once, at a recent dinner party, an Englishwoman asked me who my contemporaries were, my nearest and dearest; I had to say, after some thought, that they were all dead. I wonder if these erased people are what draw me to *Call Me Joe*, which is such an effective picture of loneliness and beauty that I want to erase the sadness I feel looking at it. There is so much accuracy in the painting, from Joe's style—familiar to me from my Brooklyn youth, when you dressed up your long john top with a brightly patterned shirt—to what Alice Neel saw in his eyes; he connects with her through a kind of shared loneliness. Paintings are as much the artist's projection of self as they are the subject's projection of an idealized self—this is who I am, but who is that? This is a painting about character in flux even as it tries to declare itself a self. Joe is, I would imagine, a teenager, and it's impossible to know how much loss—how many erasures—he'd experienced in his life by the time Neel painted him. But having grown up in the Brooklyn equivalent of East Harlem, I know Joe knew something about loss; he was colored and male and tender, and how much did that matter in the world? Especially the world he knew, which prized hardness over understanding, because understanding led to seeing and talking about and being critical of the ghetto that had made you, or tried to unmake you. Joe's mouth is sealed against many unspeakable things, including his life, which, given economics and racism, was being erased. Neel sees all that, of course, while being most alive to how life had already made this boy this particular shape—which she records through the specificity of interpretation. Reading various interviews and books about Neel, and combining all her words, I found this erasure: "I did the best I could / I could not seem to speak / But there was so much to see." And here is a poem that Neel's son, Hartley, gave me on a recent trip to his mother's studio in Stowe, Vermont: "Alice said the world treats your children as you have treated them."

Anselmo, 1962

Abdul Rahman, 1964

Abdul Rahman, 1964

James Farmer, 1964

Pregnant Maria, 1964

How does energy show itself in stillness? For the painted portrait to be achieved, the subject must arrange himself or herself in stillness, usually while sitting in a chair, or lying on a bed or sofa, all the while projecting a certain energy that could be viewed as antithetical to stillness, the energy of one's "I." The portraitist doesn't so much harness this energy as use the canvas's edges as a parameter or a benign line to frame the real world of the picture, while excluding that which does not belong. And yet the great portraitists make you wonder what else was in the room, or behind the chair the subject is sitting in. Portraits are filled with ghosts—the people the subject loves or, out of emotional necessity, has forgotten. You can't actually see any of those people, but they're there, in the subject's eyes and the artist's eyes, since each is reflected in the other.

Pregnant Maria is a study of growth in stillness. Maria is growing a life—a life neither she nor the artist yet knows. And yet they know it—it fills Maria, and makes her vibrant and still with expectation. One could write a dissertation on the dissertations that have been written about the history of pregnant women in Western and non-Western art—Mary and all those annunciations, and so on. But little has been written about the reality of transformation—Maria's body growing slowly, day after day. In Alice Neel's picture, Maria is herself and not herself; her baby is not a self, either. All of this weighs on the mind like a solid—a solid wrapped in conjecture. Neel gives us the heft of Maria's pregnancy, its awkwardness. She can't right herself, because nothing feels right to her former self, the body she knew from another lifetime. The painting is not about maternal contentment, but unease; there's an aura of jittery indecision. Pregnancy is a state that requires waiting—incubation—and what can a body do as it waits? Think about itself. Neel's portraits of women reveal an affinity, the shared understanding that she and her female subject know how to wait. But for what? The option of not being women? What do these women want? Maria's baby is pulling her into an unknown sphere, just as sitting for one's portrait is an unknown: What will the artist make of me? She is vulnerable to both her biology and to the artist simultaneously. Neel, for her part, conveys a message that only another woman and mother could recognize: how pregnancy weighs down the body, and can weigh down consciousness, too, even as the soul struggles to project its own "I."

Mother and Child, c. 1962

Hugh Hurd, 1964

The Black Boys, 1967

Black Man, 1966

Ron Kajiwara, 1971

There was a time when young artists living in New York expressed themselves as much through their art as through self-presentation; an aura of artistry surrounded their indisputable chic. Indeed, a number of those figures didn't really make much of a distinction between what they did and who they were: each made the artist. Such young people—they were always young—lived in a world where art, fashion, and publishing converged. In the 1970s, they entertained themselves over at Reno Sweeney or at the Brasserie. Their gossip was as hard as their look, which was a throwback to those Depression-era, art deco nights that Cole Porter described in his music: thin and sharp. All that Manhattan talk over cocktails, or a little blow. Then these young glittering things fluttered their hands again, and laughed—there was lots of laughter then—before moving on to another event, or more gossip. Lots of that talk had quotation marks around it, especially when it came to words or feelings such as tenderness, or hope.

When Alice Neel painted his portrait, Ron Kajiwara was a graphic designer at *Vogue*; later, he became the magazine's design director. He also designed sets for downtown theater spectacles. (*The New York Times* critic Mel Gussow once gave him a rave review, writing of a 1982 production: "The designer [of *The Dispossessed* by Leonard Melfi] is Ron Kajiwara. Remember his name if you have a loft or a play that you want decorated. . . . Mr. Kajiwara has made a substantial contribution.") Kajiwara also worked with the legendary Ronald Tavel, who scripted Warhol's first "talkies," including his 1965 film *Kitchen*, among many others. Among Kajiwara's many friends and colleagues in the downtown art scene was dancer and choreographer Stuart Pimsler, who, on the occasion of this book, wrote:

> Ron embodied the innocence of a child with the elegance and grace of an esteemed master. . . . His seemingly stark simplicity was meticulously framed in his palette of black, white, and red. His work at *Vogue* surely informed the ways in which he was able to create visual beauty through the perfect blend and balance of even the most minimal of elements. His forever-demure, soft demeanor would explode with excitement when he landed on a new place of discovery. . . . Ron and I both shared a deep love and closeness with our respective families. His parents were Japanese

immigrant farmers who had been commandeered, with Ron and his siblings, into a California internment camp during World War II. Ron was as fraught with concern about his family's opinion regarding his homosexuality as I was regarding my lower-middle-class Jewish family's opinions about my decision to become an artist.

Among their collaborations was the dance production *Sentry*, which debuted in New York in 1984. Pimsler noted that it was "inspired by a photograph Ron clipped from a magazine . . . of an injured soldier lying in a Beirut hospital. In his stark room, the heavily bandaged soldier is positioned in front of a window which is being fortified by seemingly phosphorescent red and blue sandbags. This was a quintessential Ron aesthetic touchstone—being able to uncover the hidden beauty in any environment, even one of decay and destruction."

At the time he sat for Neel, Kajiwara was at the epicenter of a new kind of show-biz hip; her portrait is as much a report about that particular New York phenomenon as it is a record of style as a way of being—a post-Whistlerian illustration of modernism at work, inherently queer, bristling with attitude and dandy distance and an almost feminine softness or yearning behind the pretend armor. In her important 1973 essay on style, Kennedy Fraser writes that the stylish "must keep leaping up and sniping at complacency. The slightest softening, or a tilt in the direction of coziness or caution, could cause the death of style." Indeed, there is a certain playfulness and hardness that Kajiwara shows in the world of this painting: a world made vertical by Neel, thus emphasizing her subject's thinness, his long hand and knee-high boots. He wears a coat that Baudelaire, one of the more original dandies, might have envied. But it's Kajiwara's left hand on his thin hip that says something—says a great deal—about attitude as a kind of defense, a not-suffering-fools-gladly dandy stance that pays back, with its archness, all those people who no doubt chided Kajiwara for his apparent difference, for the years he spent in the closet, in that internment camp, in a largely white avant-garde world. Ron wears whatever attitude he could muster with the confidence, self-interest, and slightly skeptical self-possession of an artist whose body and style amounts to one aspect of his art, while his interior life is being coaxed out, teased out, by Neel, who understood the children of her time, and how they came to be, as much as she understood anything.

Woman, 1966

Ed Sun, 1971

Ian and Mary, 1971

Carmen and Judy, 1972

In her beautiful, hard, and certain essay, "The Love of God and Affliction," the religious philosopher Simone Weil said: "The great enigma of human life is not suffering but affliction. It is not surprising that the innocent are killed, tortured, driven from their country, made destitute or reduced to slavery, imprisoned in camps or cells, since there are criminals to perform such actions." I am certain that Alice Neel, more than many an American artist, had a deep understanding of affliction. She did not use her work to escape it, but rather to plunge further into it—into the trauma of being despised, or forsaken. Indeed, if she had any credo as an artist, it was to show us ourselves, and herself, even when (or especially when) it was dangerous and hard to do so. Neel lived through two world wars, the Korean War, and the Vietnam War; she saw dictators rise and fall, and empires clash with their colonies. She knew that the first mark of being political was *looking*: seeing what was done to others in this world, and how the afflicted became afflicted, or what nowadays we might call the disenfranchised. Neel experienced affliction herself, firsthand. She lost two girls, her eldest children—one by kidnapping, essentially, and so saw the criminal at work in her personal life. What might have felled a person with lesser capabilities (and did harm Neel; in 1930, she suffered a nervous breakdown) went into the work.

Neel had art—her outlet—and the discipline of education on her side. Yet she was ambivalent about the opportunities she had because of race and class. When others describe her psychological difficulties—her proclivity for troubled partners and so on—it strikes me that it was her way of paying for what she felt was an overabundance of privilege. If she was stripped of it by feckless lovers and the like, she would be more real. Pain would be her portion; it would neutralize her tremendous gifts and make her more like other people, other women. Weil says, though, that affliction is different than pain or humiliation. Affliction, she writes, "is an uprooting of life, a more or less attenuated equivalent of death, made irresistibly present to the soul by the attack or immediate apprehension of physical pain." To live with fear, and the possibility of being annihilated at the hands of someone you have welcomed into your home, is a devastating thing—you must fight to be yourself, have yourself, let alone have the love of the people you cherish most, your children.

In Phoebe Hoban's 2010 *Alice Neel: The Art of Not Sitting Pretty* one is struck again and again by the biographer's question: Why? Why did Neel make this choice when she could have made another? I think Neel, like many powerful women, was conflicted: power was the province of men. Yet she wanted power for herself. Did that make her less a woman, to be this person who could make a world by marrying her consciousness to someone else's unconscious? (To be the subject of a painting, to pose, is to delve deep into one's unconscious; sitting encourages that, especially if the painter isn't a chatterbox.) What was a woman? Someone who withstood maleness with great forbearance? Or was turned on by its unutterable difference—the right to be violent, to act out, to take what was his. Maleness as an idea, let alone a reality, is all-pervasive. I have heard women of great intelligence and imagination mention their husbands before they say anything about themselves at all. I have loved boys whose mothers put their self-dramatization before their sons, and expected those boys to love me. I have had a mother who shared her hard-earned money with a father who didn't work and who, in fact, lived with (and to some extent off of) his own mother. I have had female siblings who condoned—by not criticizing—male relatives who dangled my boy self off balconies, and put plastic bags over my head. And then I grew up, sort of, and slept with older men who were not there, because of drink or other partners. This was what I did and what I knew and what I searched for: a kind of slightly absent authority, a protector who didn't protect, who kept the world away from me with a sharp word. I felt shipwrecked on a stony, barren island that I confused with love, because the love I knew was an out-of-control maleness—the theater of maleness that came in, dominated the scene, and then exited, stage left. Neel would have understood all that, and the aspects of her biography that are difficult for others to accept have shown up in any relationship any of us has had, if you are dealing with maleness, or the idea of it.

The point is that Neel understood Carmen and Judy. Carmen, a Haitian cleaning woman, took care of Neel's home and babysat for her daughter-in-law, Nancy. (My mother also supported herself, at times, by cleaning and babysitting.) The beatific look on Carmen's face—the look of the afflicted who feel it is morally offensive to show the world their affliction—shows herself to Neel, as her mentally challenged child looks up at that figure she cannot help but love. There is not one of us who has not been Judy—life has harmed us, injured the brain and heart, and yet there is the softness of the woman who holds us. As she does so, we imagine she holds up the world too. Judy's pudendum, Carmen's breast: these are targets that men zero in on—in many, many paintings and books, and in life—to establish their sovereignty. But what if you took that guy out of the picture? What if the conversation was between two women who shared, to some degree, a domestic space and who shared, to some degree, a different but still intense interest in the child? That's what Neel depicts in this painting too: the private space of women talking to each other about their bodies, and their female children's bodies.

Neel has the power to make us all feel less lonely in whatever roles—male and female, black and white, the powerful and the afflicted—nature and society have given us (or have tried to, at least). One sees, in Judy, Neel's curiosity about the two girl children she didn't get to raise; had her first baby, Santillana, lived past infancy, and had Isabetta not been taken from her, would she have been a different mother? The ghosts of her girl children are in this painting, made in 1972, when Neel was herself in her seventies. It took that long for her subjects here to present themselves to her, but understanding only comes when we understand. I didn't understand *Carmen and Judy* until I remembered what the world was like after *he* left, whoever he was, or whatever we called him: Papa, husband, whatever. The kitchen was filled with women and children who were not looked after or protected, except by one another. That's the thing about Neel—you really have to search your own shit, your own past, in order to glean what she was doing. My past is my past, but I borrow from *Carmen and Judy* to remember the glory in it, borne in part of my desire to survive affliction with the grace Weil describes, which is just another word for God. In the months since I've been looking at *Carmen and Judy* again, I find myself wading out past that barren island and into other waters, warm and loving, but frightening too, because of that very thing—the love that one can find, looking past the wreckage.

Kanuthia, 1973

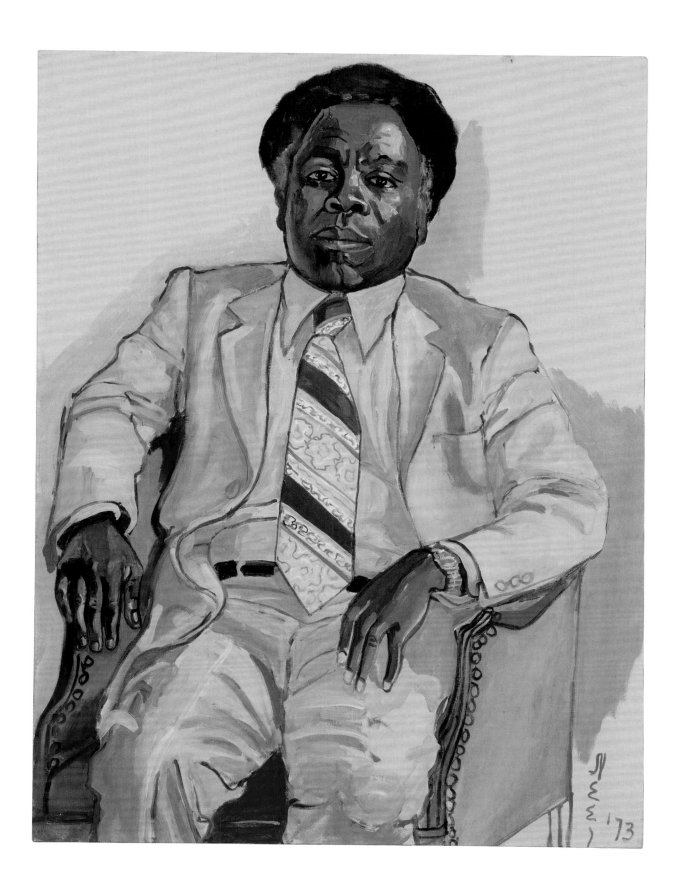

Faith Ringgold, 1977

Yumiko Okamura, 1976

The Arab, 1976

Benjamin, 1976

I have two boys myself, she said, dipping her brush in the water jar; the water turned blue and he could see her hand behind the blue. Two boys, Richard and Hartley. They're big boys now, and you'll be a big boy before you know it, too. She made some more marks on the big page—she called it a canvas—and it was like she was writing, but her marks didn't resemble the writing he did in his schoolbook, his thoughts about history or math or any part of Manhattan, his playground. The artist's gestures were bigger and filled with something he could not name. She looked at him and then she made a mark on the canvas, and then she looked at him again and made another mark. Her painting was like another conversation as she made conversation. He loved listening to her voice—it was light and cheery. It sounded the way sunlight could make you feel when you were outside, or inside a room like this one, at the artist's place, which was filled with the artist's presence. Her white hair and blue smock. She made another mark. Time passed. She said, My sons, the youngest is a doctor, and his older brother, Richard, went to law school, right up there at Columbia, and it's lonely to miss your boys when they grow up, but they are always with you because they *are* you, or part of you. I bet your mother feels that way, too. It is a privilege to know my children, a privilege to know you. Are you okay? What can I get you? A mother's work is never done—let alone a painter's! Then she laughed, that charming laugh that reminded him of young girls and the way ribbons look in sunlight, in some girl's hair—satiny like that, like something you wanted to eat.

She looked at him again, raised her brush. It's hard to say what attracts me to the people I paint, and I think that's part of it—you can't explain it in words. But I'm glad you agreed to sit. It's pleasant to be here together, isn't it, remembering my sons? I wonder if you've met. Every time I see my boys I see our history. Your mother can tell you about that. Because no matter how far away they go, you're wrapped up in your kids—as much as you're wrapped up in yourself. That's part of life, or a part of my life, and I like telling people about myself if they're willing to share themselves, for my work. Actually, I consider it *our* work: I see you, but only because you're here, showing me yourself.

She paused and dipped her brush in the water; this time the water turned brown. Do you like to draw, she asked? To make art? For me, she continued, it's a way of being—of earning the right to be alive. Because we're all here on this earth to do something, to declare ourselves and have a purpose. I can see determination in your eyes. And such beautiful softness in your shoulders. She stopped herself then, fearing she would make the child self-conscious, but she continued speaking her mind, only to herself. Alice said to Alice: Love comes in many forms, and I love you, now, while I'm painting you. That love has a certain intensity while I'm painting a person, and it may not last past the painting, but at least the work's a record of that love. My paintings are a way, sometimes, of trying to understand how we get into another person, and why, and why it's beautiful, hard, exhausting, enriching. People—that's all we have, one another. And sometimes that's unbearable, and sometimes all we crave.

On the third or fourth day he came to sit, she invited the boy to take a look at what they had done together. He did. And he was amazed and then shy and then amazed again because there he was.

Cyrus, the Gentle Iranian, 1979

Stephen Shepard, 1978

Just look at him, in all his sexy knowingness. Is he gay? I don't know, but there's that bomber jacket and those Jheri curls. Sometimes, you meet people who won't back down from their own stare. Stephen Shepard could be considered a little overly pert, maybe a little arrogant, but why would you want to do that? He's just himself. A perfect specimen of self-realization and the fun that follows when your body is open to the limitlessness of pleasure—when it's done right. Stephen's sexy standing-in-the-middle-of-life makes us feel more alive, too. He's respectful of Alice, but respectful of himself, too, and what charms and seduces more than humor and authority?

My friend Valda would have loved Stephen Shepard, this painting. We called her Mrs. Vreeland because she had so much style. In my memory of her—she's dead now, died nearly twelve years ago, something like that, why pay attention to when time stopped?—Mrs. Vreeland calls. She's talking to me. What time do you get off work? Let's go out. A phrase that means many things, including the reordering of one's expectations—exchanging the immense solitude of a book for the immense solidarity of her company. Mrs. Vreeland, in a fit of pique with a lover: Let's go out. The US being not HIM or HER but US. Mrs. Vreeland in Tribeca, or maybe on the Lower East Side, incandescent with expectation and no expectation. There are our hands, up in the air! Bohannon! Come on and do it! Do it! Do it! We lived for the bridges in "Let's Start the Dance," the best disco song ever. What's Steve Shepard doing? What's Elaine doing? (Remember them?) Elaine, on the phone: I'm working. I'm at Mr. Chow's. Mrs. Vreeland: We're going out. Elaine knows what "we" means. Elaine: It's funny, Michael Chow doesn't like non-colored people. It's weird. Mrs. Vreeland: We're going out! Elaine: Why not come here first. It's early. What is it? Eleven? Twelve? Uptown or down, depending on where we're living. (It's 1980 or 1983, and no one wants to live in New York.) Anyway, we're on our way to Mr. Chow's. Mrs. Vreeland, skinny and hungry, immaculate and made up to meet the fantasy that is New York, with its various Holly Golightlys and any number of writers. Let's split the cab, or not pay for it at all. The driver is cute. Let him know he's cute, and we won't have to pay for the cab. In the door at Mr. Chow's. Art deco everything. Our hands are up in the air! Do it! Do it! Do it! A ringside seat at Mr. Chow's.

There's Emily, there's John D looking at Emily in her party dress. That was hilarious, Emily describing herself in her party dress on the pole at Boots and Saddle. Do it. And then there's Elaine, chasing Emily while Steve Shepard looks on, walking by. Oh, yes, that's the way it is, and the way everything should be. Do it. Mrs. Vreeland: a little trip to the powder room. She returns; suddenly, she's above it all. Her vodka gimlet, untouched. But there's Bohannon, making us feel things. Do it! Do it! Do it! Bohannon speaks/sings: "It's not a question of getting down, but actually how low you can go. Make it funky." Can we make it funky? Mrs. Vreeland's red lips, and then a sentence: What did you do last night? Hilton: I went to a party. Mrs. Vreeland: And? Hilton: Well, it was a black party, so there was lots of Lanolin and coconut oil. Mrs. Vreeland: I know those smells! Do it! Do it! Do it! Mrs. Vreeland, a cloud of perfection in her cloud of what she calls "dummy face powder" and European manners. A little chicken now for our little supper, maybe a little fish? She wants the rituals of "normalcy"—dinner with a companion—but she doesn't want to observe those rituals when she doesn't feel like it. Why should we pay for this? . . . There's a man, he likes us, oh! Don't be like that, old man! Suddenly Mrs. Vreeland is Louise Brooks, black hair helmeted and careless in the twentieth-century way, which is to say everything matters to her, and some things don't. The old man is a professor, someone Hilton knows from Amsterdam, a city he loves for a time, a city of hope. Canals. Hilton, hi hi hi! says the Professor, not taking his eyes off Mrs. Vreeland, Hilton's companion; she'll take his call in the morning. Hi! Oh, can't we do it?! Do it?! Do it?! Bohannon: "The deeper you go, the more you know." Back in the cab, Elaine on the jump seat (remember those?): down to Save the Robots, down to see Darryl, down to see Steve Shepard. We're going out! What's Akure doing? And Wanda? Oh, let's just do it! Do it! Do it! our bodies say as Bohannon tells us what to do, the remnants of Mrs. Vreeland's dummy face powder crystalizing in what we haven't swallowed of the just left New York nighttime air, with and without Stephen.

List of Works

People on Steps, 1952
Pencil on paper
10¾ × 14 inches
27.3 × 35.6 cm
The Estate of Alice Neel
Page 12

Girl with Pink Flower, 1940s
Oil on canvas
24⅛ × 17⅞ inches
61.3 × 45.4 cm
The Estate of Alice Neel
Page 19

Baby on Blue Sofa, 1939–1940
Oil on canvas
15⅛ × 24⅞ inches
38.4 × 63.2 cm
The Estate of Alice Neel
Page 20

Two Girls in Spanish Harlem, 1941
Watercolor on paper
20⅞ × 15½ inches
53 × 39.4 cm
Schomburg Center for Research in
Black Culture, Art and Artifacts
Division. The New York Public
Library, Astor, Lenox and Tilden
Foundations
Page 21

Julie and the Doll, 1943
Oil on canvas
28⅛ × 20¼ inches
71.4 × 51.4 cm
The Estate of Alice Neel
Page 22

The Spanish Family, 1943
Oil on canvas
34 × 28 inches
86.4 × 71.1 cm
The Estate of Alice Neel
Page 27

T.B. Harlem, 1940
Oil on canvas
30 × 30 inches
76.2 × 76.2 cm
National Museum of Women in
the Arts, Washington, DC. Gift of
Wallace and Wilhelmina Holladay
Page 29

Building in Harlem, c. 1945
Oil on canvas
34 × 24⅛ inches
86.4 × 61.3 cm
The Estate of Alice Neel
Page 30

Armando Perez, 1945
Oil on canvas
30 × 24½ inches
76.2 × 62.2 cm
The Estate of Alice Neel
Page 35

Horace Cayton, 1949
Oil on canvas
30¼ × 24 inches
76.8 × 61 cm
The Estate of Alice Neel
Page 37

Ballet Dancer, 1950
Oil on canvas
20⅛ × 42⅛ inches
51.1 × 107 cm
Hall Collection
Pages 38–39

Rudolph Christian, 1951
Oil on canvas
30¼ × 24⅛ inches
76.8 × 61.3 cm
Private Collection
Page 41

Georgie Arce, 1955
Oil on canvas
25 × 15 inches
63.5 × 38.1 cm
Collection of William T. Hillman
Page 42

Georgie, 1950
Ink on paper
11½ × 8½ inches
29.2 × 21.6 cm
The Estate of Alice Neel
Page 45

Georgie Arce, 1952
Ink and gouache on paper
13⅞ × 10⅞ inches
35.2 × 27.6 cm
Collection John Cheim
Page 46

Georgie Arce, 1953
Oil on canvas
38 × 28 inches
96.5 × 71.1 cm
The Estate of Alice Neel
Page 47

A Spanish Boy, 1955
Oil on canvas
20½ × 27 inches
52.1 × 68.6 cm
Museum of the City of New York
Page 49

Georgie Arce, 1955
Ink on paper
8¾ × 11½ inches
22.2 × 29.2 cm
Private Collection
Page 50

Georgie Arce, 1959
Oil on canvas
36 × 25 inches
91.4 × 63.5 cm
The Estate of Alice Neel
Page 51

Georgie, 1958
Ink on paper
11½ × 8¾ inches
29.2 × 22.2 cm
The Estate of Alice Neel
Page 53

Georgie Arce No. 2, 1955
Oil on canvas
30 × 22 inches
76.2 × 55.9 cm
Private Collection
Page 55

Alice Childress, 1950
Oil on canvas
30⅛ × 20⅛ inches
76.5 × 51.1 cm
Collection of Art Berliner
Page 56

Spanish Woman, c. 1950
Oil on canvas
38 × 22 inches
96.5 × 55.9 cm
Private Collection. Courtesy
Robert Miller Gallery, New York
Page 61

Black Spanish-American Family, 1950
Oil on canvas
30 × 22 inches
76.2 × 55.9 cm
Private Collection, Chicago
Page 63

Harold Cruse, c. 1950
Oil on canvas
31 × 22 inches
78.7 × 55.9 cm
The Estate of Alice Neel
Page 64

Two Girls, 1954
Ink and gouache on paper
29¼ × 21½ inches
74.3 × 54.6 cm
Private Collection. Courtesy
Robert Miller Gallery, New York
Page 70

Mercedes Arroyo, 1952
Oil on canvas
25 × 24⅛ inches
63.5 × 61.3 cm
Daryl and Steven Roth
Page 67

Young Woman, 1956
Ink on paper
13¾ × 11 inches
34.9 × 27.9 cm
Private Collection
Page 74

Three Puerto Rican Girls, 1955
Oil on canvas
32 × 28 inches
81.3 × 71.1 cm
Private Collection
Page 68

Nurse, 1954
Pencil on paper on cardboard
13⅞ × 10⅞ inches
35.2 × 27.6 cm
The Estate of Alice Neel
Page 75

Two Puerto Rican Boys, 1956
Oil on canvas
32 × 28 inches
81.3 × 71.1 cm
Jeff and Mei Sze Greene Collection
Page 69

Rita and Hubert, 1958
Oil on canvas
34 × 40 inches
86.4 × 101.6 cm
Defares Collection
Page 77

Two Girls, Spanish Harlem, 1959
Oil on canvas
30 × 25 inches
76.2 × 63.5 cm
Museum of Fine Arts, Boston.
Gift of Barbara Lee
Page 79

Abdul Rahman, 1964
Oil on canvas
20 × 16 inches
50.8 × 40.6 cm
The Estate of Alice Neel
Page 89

Call Me Joe, 1955
Oil on canvas
34 × 22 inches
86.4 × 55.9 cm
Private Collection. Courtesy
Michael Rosenfeld Gallery, New York
Page 80

James Farmer, 1964
Oil on canvas
43¾ × 30¼ inches
111.1 × 76.8 cm
National Portrait Gallery, Smithsonian
Institution, Washington, DC. Gift of Hartley
Neel and Richard Neel
Page 91

Anselmo, 1962
Oil on canvas
30 × 22 inches
76.2 × 55.9 cm
The Estate of Alice Neel
Page 85

Pregnant Maria, 1964
Oil on canvas
32 × 47 inches
81.3 × 119.4 cm
Private Collection
Page 92

Mother and Child, c. 1962
Oil on canvas
40⅛ × 27¼ inches
101.9 × 69.2 cm
Private Collection
Page 95

Abdul Rahman, 1964
Oil on canvas
46 × 34⅛ inches
116.8 × 86.7 cm
The Estate of Alice Neel
Page 87

Hugh Hurd, 1964
Oil on canvas
40 × 30⅛ inches
101.6 × 76.5 cm
Crystal Bridges Museum of
American Art, Bentonville, Arkansas
Page 97

Woman, 1966
Oil on canvas
46 × 31 inches
116.8 × 78.7 cm
Private Collection, Miami
Page 107

The Black Boys, 1967
Oil on canvas
46¼ × 40 inches
117.5 × 101.6 cm
The Tia Collection
Page 99

Ed Sun, 1971
Oil on canvas
42 × 30 inches
106.7 × 76.2 cm
The Estate of Alice Neel
Page 108

Black Man, 1966
Oil on canvas
44 × 28⅛ inches
111.8 × 71.4 cm
The Estate of Alice Neel
Page 101

Ian and Mary, 1971
Oil on canvas
46 × 50 inches
116.8 × 127 cm
The Estate of Alice Neel
Page 109

Ron Kajiwara, 1971
Oil on canvas
67⅞ × 35⅛ inches
172.4 × 89.2 cm
The Estate of Alice Neel
Page 102

Carmen and Judy, 1972
Oil on canvas
40 × 30 inches
101.6 × 76.2 cm
Oklahoma City Museum of Art.
Westheimer Family Collection
Page 110

Kanuthia, 1973
Oil on canvas
40 × 30 inches
101.6 × 76.2 cm
The Estate of Alice Neel
Page 115

Benjamin, 1976
Acrylic on board
29⅞ × 20¾ inches
75.9 × 52.7 cm
The Estate of Alice Neel
Page 122

Faith Ringgold, 1977
Oil on canvas
48 × 36 inches
121.9 × 91.4 cm
Exxon Mobil Corporation,
Irving, Texas
Page 117

Cyrus, the Gentle Iranian, 1979
Oil on canvas
39⅞ × 30⅛ inches
101.3 × 76.5 cm
The Estate of Alice Neel
Page 127

Yumiko Okamura, 1976
Ink on paper
40 × 25 inches
101.6 × 63.5 cm
The Estate of Alice Neel
Page 119

Stephen Shepard, 1978
Oil on canvas
32 × 24 inches
81.3 × 61 cm
The Estate of Alice Neel
Page 128

The Arab, 1976
Oil on canvas
44⅛ × 32⅛ inches
112.1 × 81.6 cm
Cantor Arts Center at Stanford
University. Museum purchase
made possible by the Robert and
Ruth Halperin Foundation
Page 121

Acknowledgments

David Zwirner and Victoria Miro wish to thank The Estate of Alice Neel, Ginny and Hartley Neel, Richard Neel, Jeremy Lewison, and Bellatrix Hubert for making the exhibitions possible. We are most grateful to Hilton Als, whose singular vision and profound understanding of Alice Neel—artist and individual—are at the heart of this exhibition. His remarkable, multifaceted writing for this publication illuminates Neel's art, in all its generosity and complexity.

The gallery would like to specially acknowledge the institutional and private lenders who loaned works from their collections for the exhibition: Art Berliner, Cantor Arts Center at Stanford University, John Cheim, Jeff and Mei Sze Greene, Hall Collection, William T. Hillman, Daryl and Steven Roth, and The Tia Collection, and those who wish to remain anonymous.

For their assistance throughout the project we are also grateful to Aurel Scheibler, Johannes Bischoff, and Oksana Shestaka of Aurel Scheibler; Xavier Hufkens and Elisabeth Van Caelenberge of Xavier Hufkens; Randy White of Robert Miller Gallery; Michael Allen, Stephanie Biron, Maryse Brand, Katie Clifford, Heather Harmon, Andrea Robertson, Dennis Santella, and Laura Finlay Smith.

Thank you to everyone at David Zwirner who contributed to the exhibition, especially Alexandra Whitney and Kelly Reynolds for shepherding this project, as well as Justin Anderson, Maggie Bamberg, Myles Bisi, Kyle Combs, Ryan Flores, Tim Gentles, Marina Gluckman, Brent Harada, Rebecca Holmberg, David King, Elizabeth Koehn, Sam Greenleaf Miller, Clive Murphy, Britta Nelson, Mike Schreiber, Emily Shanahan, Louise Sørensen, and Aengus Woods.

For the design of this catalogue, we extend our appreciation to Laura Lindgren. For their help with its preparation, thanks are furthermore due to Rebecca Ashby-Colón, Dan Bradica, Hope Dickens, Anna Drozda, Doro Globus, Julia Joern, Molly Stein, Jules Thomson, Anne Wehr, and Lucas Zwirner.

Thank you to everyone at Victoria Miro who contributed to the exhibition and publication, especially Glenn Scott Wright and Erin Manns, as well as Martin Coomer, Marisa J. Futernick, Jon Glazier, Adeline Guy, Emma Mee, Oliver Miro, Kathy Stephenson, Rachel Taylor, Hannah van den Wijngaard, David Wood, and Isabelle Young.

Co-published by David Zwirner Books and Victoria Miro
on the occasion of

Alice Neel, Uptown
David Zwirner, 525 and 533 West 19th Street, New York
February 23–April 22, 2017

Victoria Miro, 16 Wharf Road, London
May 18–July 29, 2017

Curated by Hilton Als

David Zwirner Books
529 West 20th Street, 2nd Floor
New York, New York 10011
+1 212 727 2070
davidzwirnerbooks.com

Victoria Miro
16 Wharf Road
London N1 7RW
+44 20 7336 8109
victoria-miro.com

Editors: Hilton Als, Lucas Zwirner
Project Managers: Doro Globus, Anne Wehr
Project Assistant: Molly Stein
Proofreader: Anna Drozda

Design: Laura Lindgren
Photography Coordinator: Hope Dickens
Production Manager: Jules Thomson
Color Separations: VeronaLibri, Verona
Printing: VeronaLibri, Verona

Typeface: Jauría
Paper: Périgord, 170 gsm

Photography
Dan Bradica: pp. 12, 42, 67, 97, 101, 115
Photograph © 2017 Museum of Fine Arts, Boston: p. 79
Ethan Palmer: cover, pp. 19, 22, 35, 53, 64, 85, 95, 107, 108,
122, 127
Adam Reich: p. 119
Lee Stalsworth: p. 29
Malcolm Varon: pp. 27, 37, 51, 63, 75, 77

Publication © 2017 David Zwirner Books / Victoria Miro

"The Other New York" © 2017 Jeremy Lewison
Texts by Hilton Als © 2017 Hilton Als

All artwork © 2017 The Estate of Alice Neel

David Zwirner Books edition
    ISBN 978-1-941701-60-7
    LCCN 2017933252

Distributed in the United States and Canada by
ARTBOOK | D.A.P.
75 Broad Street, Suite 630
New York, New York 10004
artbook.com

Distributed in Asia, Australia, Middle East,
South Africa, and South America by
Thames & Hudson, Ltd.
181A High Holborn
London WC1V 7QX
thamesandhudson.com

Victoria Miro edition
    ISBN 978-0-9934420-3-2

Distributed in Europe by
Cornerhouse Publications
2 Tony Wilson Place
Manchester M15 4FN
cornerhousepublications.org

Cover: *Harold Cruse*, c. 1950 (detail)
Page 4: *Building in Harlem*, c. 1945 (detail)
Pages 10–11: *The Black Boys*, 1967 (detail)